T0292537

PERFECT IN US

Vincent Giddens

Perfect IN US

iUniverse books may be ordered through booksellers or by contacting:

iUniverse
1663 Liberty Drive
Bloomington, IN 47403
www.iuniverse.com
1-800-Authors (1-800-288-4677)

ISBN: 978-1-5320-9162-9 (sc)
ISBN: 978-1-5320-9827-7 (hc)
ISBN: 978-1-5320-9163-6 (e)

Library of Congress Control Number: 2020901482

Print information available on the last page.

iUniverse rev. date: 03/19/2020

PERFECT IN US

Max's 9th birthday was coming up and he was finally beginning to feel older. His parents were always letting his older brother Dray do "big kid" things, but he could tell they were beginning to trust him more and more.

Sometimes at school, he felt pressured from other kids to do what was "cool" or popular, but he also knew some of those things didn't feel like the right choice.

For as long as he could remember, his parents had told him, "God wants us to always choose love - to be kind to others and lift them up instead of tearing them down. Always treat others the way you'd want to be treated."

Later that morning at school, Max's teacher introduced a new kid to the class. His family had just moved to town from Florida. Max wondered how far away that was.

He also had a Mohawk, which Max thought was pretty cool. He seemed a little shy. Max could imagine how it felt to be in a new place where everything is different.

He wondered if the new kid had friends he had to leave behind in Florida...

Max looked forward to recess every day at school. He could finally talk and laugh with his classmates! He even got to meet kids from other classes on the playground. It was Max's favorite part of the day. When recess finally came that afternoon, Max looked around the playground and spotted the new kid playing on the monkey bars. Max liked the monkey bars too and ran over to join him. Just as he arrived at the monkey bars, their classmate Dajus, walked up behind them. Max knew Dajus was a bit of a bully - he was always getting in trouble for talking back to their teacher.

"Is he your friend, Max?" Dajus asked, with a smirk.

"I don't know him yet. He's new here..." said Max.

Dajus replied, "Well, don't play with him... his clothes are funny, and he has crazy hair!" Dajus laughed as he ran away to play with the other kids.

Max looked at the new kid. He had heard their conversation and his eyes were welling up with tears. The bell rang to tell everyone recess was over. The new kid quickly wiped the tears away and headed back into the building.

Max's mom picked him up from school at the end of the day. Max stared out the window thinking about what had happened at recess.

"Max, you have been quiet this evening. Did something happen at school?"

"I'm okay, just thinking..." said Max.

When they arrived at home, Max's dad was waiting at the door for a bear hug. Dray gave Max a light punch on the arm.

They always ate dinner together as a family. That night, they were trying something new. Dray had never tried it before and he wanted something familiar.

"It's good!" said Max.

Their parents, almost in unison, pleaded for Dray to at least try some.

Max finally spoke up about what had been bothering him all afternoon.

"Hey, Dad... Dajus asked me not to play with the new kid at school because he is different."

Their dad replied, "Boys, we are all different on the outside, what's on the inside is what makes you special. When you are confused or you need help, you can say a prayer that gives you access to your special powers – the Spirit of God that lives in us. The Spirit can give you love, courage and many other super powers."

"Even strength?" Max asked.

"Yes, Max." His dad responded.

"The Armor of God will protect you in the face of fear! Your mother and I were nine years old the first time we said the prayer..."

"I will be nine tomorrow." Max said.

After sitting for a while with a scowl on his face, Dray snuck a taste of the meal. Instantly, his frown changed to a smile as he took another bite.

Max fell back in his chair.

"Aw, I was going to ask for his!"

The family laughed.

That weekend was Max's birthday celebration at the arcade. When Max and Dray arrived, they looked for their friends. Surprisingly, the new kid from Max's class was also there, standing cowardly in the corner. He didn't seem to have any friends around.

Max thought about the prayer.

"That's the new kid from my class. Dajus said not to play with him, but everyone needs a friend. Will you pray with me, Dray?" asked Max.

Together they prayed, "...As we put on the Armor of God!"

The boys were suddenly overcome with the Spirit. Max felt the courage he needed to invite the new kid to join his party.

The new kid felt an awesome presence from them unlike anything he had ever felt before.

Max finally feels like a big kid.

Max feels perfect.

1 John 4:12 - No man has seen God at any time. If we love one another, God dwells in us, and His love is perfected in us.

American King James Version

Thank You!